The Pharmaceutical Sales Representative Handbook

A Field Handbook for All Current and Future Pharmaceutical Sales Representatives

The Pharmaceutical Sales Representative Handbook

A Field Handbook for All Current and Future Pharmaceutical Sales Representatives

By
Todd Bearden
And
Larry Martin

iUniverse, Inc.
New York Bloomington

The Pharmaceutical Sales Representative Handbook

A Field Handbook for All Current and Future Pharmaceutical Sales Representatives

Copyright © 2008 by Todd Bearden and Larry Martin

All rights reserved. No part of this book may be used or reproduced by any means, graphic, electronic, or mechanical, including photocopying, recording, taping or by any information storage retrieval system without the written permission of the publisher except in the case of brief quotations embodied in critical articles and reviews.

iUniverse books may be ordered through booksellers or by contacting:

iUniverse
1663 Liberty Drive
Bloomington, IN 47403
www.iuniverse.com
1-800-Authors (1-800-288-4677)

Because of the dynamic nature of the Internet, any Web addresses or links contained in this book may have changed since publication and may no longer be valid. The views expressed in this work are solely those of the author and do not necessarily reflect the views of the publisher, and the publisher hereby disclaims any responsibility for them.

ISBN: 978-1-4401-0945-4 (pbk)
ISBN: 978-1-4401-0946-1 (ebk)

Printed in the United States of America

iUniverse rev. date: 11/10/2008

Introduction

We have all seen those sharp looking young men and women breeze into our doctor's office with their little black wheel bags. They usually greet the receptionist with a smile and head straight back in to the doctors' area. Who are they? What are they up to? And Why?

They are pharmaceutical sales representatives -- the sales reps. They are out in front of a 200 billion dollar industry that, for all its trumpeted failings, has the focused goal of keeping well people well, or making sick people better. And this being America, the companies are doing business for profit and in the face of very stiff competition, the kind of regulated competition that in other industries gives us safer and better aircraft and safer and better food. This industry, the so-called Big Pharma, touches one way or another most Americans with cutting edge medicines that turn despair into hope, and add quality to the lives of countless millions. But like any huge American industry, it is under frequent attack in books, the media, and even the occasional movie. Some of the attacks against the industry have at their core reasonable justification, and changes have been effected as a result. Others may seem a little gratuitous, as if the very size of the industry and the command it has on all our lives is itself justification for the attacks. But regardless of the level of criticism of the industry, though constantly adapting, it is here to stay. And as long as America remains a market economy, there will be challenging jobs for sales reps in this industry.

There are at any given time about a hundred thousand sales reps in the field, all selected through a highly competitive process, and all well compensated by their companies. At the same time, however, pharmaceutical sales is a vigorously merit-based profession, and only the most productive young men and women will survive and thrive. If it seems that the ubiquitous sales rep is something new to the universe of health care, it's because all of these new medicines are, indeed, something new. Pharmaceuticals has transformed from an industry that was pretty much limited to aspirin and a few sulfa drugs and "patent medicines" in our grandfathers' days, to an industry that is coping with Research & Development (R&D) and clinical successes to the point that it has had to create a new class, an altogether new type of employee for its sales force. Consider that the Pharmaceutical Research and Manufacturers of America (PhRMA) estimate that there are currently 2000 new medicine compounds in the late stages of clinical development. These medicines will be available soon; and many of them will treat diseases and conditions currently considered untreatable.

It is for this reason that Big Pharma seeks out the best educated and motivated young men and women on university American campuses and U.S. military out-processing centers every year. They are looking for the best people to explain the new medicines to physicians who no longer have the luxury of time to do their own research on the increasingly complex world of pharmaceuticals. If you think otherwise, just ask any physician if he has time to keep up will all the journals, treat his patients, deal with insurance matters, and have a life.

The pharmaceutical industry will spend great time, energy and financial resources to train and prepare its sales force to represent its products. Sales rep training is not limited to developing an intimate knowledge of the products, but also devotes a significant amount of time on preparing its sales force to operate under the highest ethical standards, as governed by PhRMA, Code on Interactions with Healthcare Professionals. The hundred thousand or so sales reps in the field today are operating under the strictest professional and ethical guidelines associated with any industry in America. The products and the rules of conduct are constantly upgrading, as is the cutting edge of the industry, its sales force.

This handbook is designed for the current and future Pharmaceutical Sales Representative; it is a quick reference guide, a field manual that can be referred to for many of the situations that sales reps encounter in a given day. It was written by reps for reps. It is not intended to help you land your next job in pharmaceutical sales, it is, rather, designed to help you excel in your current job as a sales rep. It is a battle handbook that can be used on a daily basis in navigating the many situations reps will encounter. It discusses the ins and outs of the job with a "real world" perspective. Its goal is simple; to give you a head start, and to keep you out in front in the world of pharmaceutical sales. It will create a uniform approach to many of the situations you will face everyday, from how to approach an office for the first time to handling your most challenging customers. It is a compilation of the best practices, techniques and procedures taken from the authors' thirty-five years of field experience in the industry, and is intended for the development of field reps and their use as a daily pocket guide, carried to the field everyday and referred to in office waiting rooms before and after a call. It was designed with you in mind. Small enough to carry in your sales bag, yet versatile enough to read in waiting rooms or your company car between calls. In this little book we have developed the "ten rules to live by" for reps. Interwoven in greater detail in each chapter, these rules up front will provide you with quick reference on short notice.

1. Give 110% and then some each and every day.
2. Always be ethical in everything you do.
3. Never lie to a customer. If you do not know the answer, go find it and follow up.
4. Be professional and look professional at all times.
5. Strive to learn as much about this great industry as you can.
6. Be a leader, be a volunteer, be PASSIONATE.
7. Go above and beyond in your training.
8. Remember, you are a guest in a customers office, treat everyone with respect.
9. Listen more than you talk.
10. Become an asset to your customers.

Now that we have given you a small taste of what is to come, use this handbook to go from average to great, from the middle of the pack to the top of the sales force and well on your way to Presidents Cup year after year.

Contents

Introduction.. i

1 - Training: From The Home Office To The Field 1

2 - In The Field (Finally) 11

3. -Planning, Targeting, Routing And Sales Reports............. 17

4. -.Why Should They See You; How To Distinguish Yourself From The Pack... 27

5. -Field Rides With Your District Manager........................ 33

6. - Meetings: POD, District Or Other............................... 43

7. - The Call: 30 Second Detail To Full Presentation, "How to do this in the real world".. 53

8. - Going The Extra Mile 63

9. - Surviving In A Changing Environment........................ 71

10. - The future.. 77

Authors: Todd Bearden and Larry Martin 83

Acronyms 85

Chapter 1

Training: From The Home Office To The Field

Once you land your job as a Pharmaceutical Sales Representative, training begins immediately. Most pharmaceutical companies start each new representative out with a home study period usually lasting three to four weeks. This phase will be stressful for a person who has never been in a tough, competitive training environment. To get a leg up for this phase of training, we have compiled a few critical success tips.

- ☐ **Have a plan.** Your company will expect you to follow their study plan. Most companies expect you to be studying about eight hours a day. Consider those eight hours a minimum.

- ☐ **Get ahead in the schedule.** If the company expects you to cover 2 – 3 chapters a day, cover four. This way, if you have any difficulty with any of the subject matter, you have built yourself a cushion.

- ☐ **Communicate with your mentor or trainer.** Do not close yourself in. Call your trainer or mentor if you have a problem with the subject matter. Better to get it right at home than to struggle at On Site training.

- ☐ **Communicate with your new team mates in training.** Find out who else is in the same phase of training with you and hook up with them. (Get a list of voice mail extensions from your trainer or mentor.) This type of lateral communication is usually encouraged. You can set up study sessions with your training team mates and share tips on your progress during the home study phase.

- ☐ **Take written or online exams on time.** Many home study training programs have progress checks and online written exams. Some may be multiple choice; others may be fill in the blanks or short answers. Make sure to stay in touch with your trainer or mentor on what to expect and what subject matter to focus on.

- ☐ **Pass all of your home study exams with a 90% or higher.** Pharmaceutical companies expect you to pass all home study and on site exams with a 90% or higher score. To achieve this, you'll have to dedicate yourself to study. The bottom line in this bottom line business is that the company expects you to succeed. That is why they hired you.

☐ **Avoid the distractions of the home office.** Reps work out of their home office. This includes home study. This will be a huge change if in the past you've worked side by side with your co-workers in an office setting. To minimize distractions for the eight hours of daily home study, you have to find what works best for you. If that means locking yourself in your home for eight hours, with hourly breaks, do that. For others that can be difficult. It might be easier to get out of the house and go to Barnes and Noble or a local library to study. There is no fixed solution. As long as you meet the standards and are keeping up with the schedule keep doing it your way.

One of the biggest challenges for new reps is sticking to a schedule, digging in, and getting the home study done. To assist in this area, we have inserted a table that provides an example of how a rep can get through the home study successfully and be completely prepared for the next phase of the training, the On Site Phase.

Table 1: Home Study Guide for representatives

Week ___	Morning	Afternoon	Evening	Tests
Monday				
Tuesday				
Wednesday				
Thursday				
Friday				

Now that you have completed the home study phase of your training, your next challenge is <u>on site training</u>, usually at a location selected by your Home Office Training Department. All of your time and effort put into home study will come together here. It is a time of assessment and observation by the training department on how well you have performed to date. Every pharmaceutical company has a training department composed of former field managers and field reps who have been successful in their field careers. The organization has entrusted them to guide the sales force through all training phases: new hire sales training, management development training, new product launch training, and other quarterly, annual or bi-annual training meetings. During this phase, you will live at the training site, adhere to the standards of the training department, and be prepared to pass all initial entry assessment exams that will be administered. This is excellent opportunity for a new rep to test his or her skills, meet new friends, and launch in an amazing industry of unlimited opportunities. It is also an opportunity to get off on the wrong foot and, yes, to fail. The following tips, techniques and procedures will help you avoid common pitfalls of reps.

- ☐ **Plan ahead.** Near the end of your home study period, you will be notified to prepare for your on site training. Make your travel arrangements right away. Do not wait until the last minute, or you'll be explaining to your trainers why you were not able to complete the most fundamental task – showing up on time. If in doubt about anything, communicate with your trainer, mentor or district manager. Most pharmaceutical companies require their reps to make their travel arrangement on-line. When making your initial travel arrangements, take the time to set up a profile in the travel system. It will be handy for future travel. One of the best tips we ever received was to make a checklist of what we needed to do prior to departing for on site training. The following table is an example checklist.

Table 2: Travel checklist for on site training.

To Do	Complete	Incomplete
1. Make flight reservations	X	
2. Complete all assignments and tests	X	
3. Organize all study materials (make a binder or use a folder)	X	
4. Make a packing list and lay everything out *(refer to table 3 for sample packing list)*	X	
5. Drop off clothes at the cleaners	X	
6. Get a haircut	X	
7. Call trainer a few days before departure to make sure there is no new information.	X	
8. Go over everything the day before to make sure nothing was left out (tip: check it, recheck it and check it again)	X	

☐ **Pack well.** One of the most common mistakes reps make is *over* packing for on site training. Training departments will have a dress code. It is normally *business casual.* Pack one set of clothes per day. A normal training day will begin at 8 AM and end around 5 PM. Unless there is an evening activity, after classes end you are on your own. There is no need to change into a new set of clothes if you are going out to dinner after class; however, you may want to pack one extra set of clothes just in case. Remember, this is a guide; the key is to limit your number of bags to one medium or large suitcase. This will get you through the week and you can use the weekend to get ready for the following week of training. Try to limit yourself to two pairs of dress shoes, one pair of recreational footwear and one pair of athletic shoes for physical fitness. Table 3 offers an example of a packing list for a week of training.

Table 3: Sample Packing List

Item	Number	Complete
Dress shirts	5	
Dress pants / skirts	5	
Jeans	1	
T-shirts	5	
Dress socks / hose	5 Pair	
Athletic socks	3 Pair	
Belts	2	
Dress shoes / heels	2 Pair (one tan, one black)	
Recreational shoes	1 Pair	
Athletic shoes	1 Pair	
Athletic wear	3	
Pajamas	1 set	
Toiletries	1 small travel case	
Shoe shine kit	1 small kit	

☐ **Business casual.** As stated earlier, most pharmaceutical companies have a business casual dress code for on site training. There is confusion on the meaning of business casual, so here is a guide to help you look sharp, not to over or under dress. Now, let's make sure you have the right clothing. The basic principles of business casual apply to both male and female representation.

- **Guys.** A nice pair of slacks or khakis will be appropriate for each day of training. Stick to basic colors, black, grey, brown, tan or blue. Make sure they are pressed or bring slacks that have a permanent crease or are wrinkle free. You can always run an iron over them in the morning. Avoid pants that are worn or look like they have been lurking in the bottom of your suitcase. Have a good fit - not too tight or too loose. You might want to get fitted at a men's department so you know your correct size. If your company has a jeans day, wear jeans that are free of holes and follow the same principles for slacks. Stay under the radar screen; do not bring unnecessary attention to yourself through off beat dress. Use common sense and you'll be fine.

- **Ladies.** More than once we have heard stories about "inappropriate dress". You decide what that means. But understand this is the last place you want to draw attention. When in doubt, go for the conservative. You are presenting yourself as a professional. Dress the part. Remember to take clothes that are easily dry cleaned, and do not require special handling. If you are in training for several weeks, it will be impossible to pack enough clothes to have a new outfit each day. You'll have to cycle them through the dry cleaners. Stick to the example in *Table 3* and you'll be fine.

- [ ] **Be ready for day 1.** You have arrived at On Site training, checked in to the hotel, met your roommate, if you have one, and are making sure you are ready for the first day. Some training departments will require all new reps to undergo an initial assessment to make sure their work during home study has prepared them for on site training. Come prepared for this assessment. Your trainer will prepare you. However, do not assume that any pre-tests you took will be the same as the initial assessment. We have seen new reps sent home or submitted for review by the training department because they did not pass their initial assessment exam.

- [ ] **Be mentally present.** The training department staff put a lot of time and effort in to making sure that your training will be the best to prepare you for the field. There is nothing worse than looking around in a room full of reps and noticing that some of your class mates are not mentally present for the day. Do not read newspapers during class time, text message your friends or have sidebar conversations while an instructor is presenting. Be an active participant and an active listener at all times. It surprises no one that the reps who actively participate in training are always the ones who are later on the top of the leader board or brought up on stage for outstanding sales recognition. What you do in training is what you will do in the field.

Think of The Army's motto, *"You train the way you fight"*. It works everywhere.

- ☐ **Network.** On Site training affords you the opportunity to meet people associated with management and training. Do not be afraid to introduce yourself. After you return home from training, stay in touch by email or voice mail, and be sure to thank them for their help. Your paths will cross again.

- ☐ **Be A Volunteer.** The training department works hard to present information that will prepare you for the field. One of the best ways to test that training is to volunteer at times to role play with one of the instructors or to lead a discussion group at your table. Do not over volunteer; however, it is a good idea to step up in front of the group at least a couple of times during your training. If you perform well in front of a room full of your peers, you might be prepared to do the same thing in front of your customer. Do not be guilty of never stepping up to the plate.

- ☐ **Dos and Don'ts.** Never forget that you are constantly being evaluated and judged. Be cautious of humor and profanity. Neither travel well. Just be professional at all times and you will be fine.

Chapter wrap. On Site training can be a challenge. Preparation is key. This is *your job* and you are now, formally, representing the company. Conduct yourself as a professional at all times, but especially so when you get into your territory. The old adage, *"You get out of it what you put into it"* is true. If you are prepared things may go easy; if you're not, there will be problems. Use common sense, work hard and you will be fine.

Chapter 2

In The Field (Finally)

You have finished your training and think you know everything there is to know about selling your products. Maybe not!

Most companies will have you start your "field" ride with a trainer, a POD, or cylinder mate for the first few days; introducing you as the "new" rep marketing their product, "CUREALL". This usually prompts the doctor to think, "Oh my God, not another rep!" From this moment on, how you organize, plan and execute your corporate strategy will determine your degree of success in this business. This chapter is not designed to guide you in setting up your home office or your detail bag. That's up to you and your District Manager. This chapter is a guide for your first trip in your new territory. You have completed all your field rides with your trainer and teammates and are ready to solo. Let's go!

Day 1. Planning your day is critical. Let us assume you have a route established with the help of your counterparts and today is your first day out there alone. Here are the logistic demands:

- ☐ **Maps.** Get a bundle of maps covering every zip code in your territory. Your company permitting, buy the latest map software of your territory and load it into your computer. You may want to invest in a GPS navigation system, as well. Properly used this will speed up getting to know your routing. Plan your route with efficiency in mind – how do I cover the geography. The industry standard is 8-10 physician calls per day, but don't expect to meet that standard your first time out. You'll reach that standard after a couple of outings, provided you start off with efficiency in mind.

- ☐ **Planning.** Plan your day the night before. In the beginning, you may not have any appointments or physician Lunch and Learns on your calendar. You might only be getting to know where you are going and what physicians you are going to call on that day. You can use your company's software program to set your schedule; you can use Microsoft Outlook or you can even write out on a piece of paper all the doctors you are going to see that day.

- ☐ **Preparation.** Load your samples, sales materials, and patient education information in your car the night before. Gas up your company car! Don't wait until the morning you leave. This keeps you at home, not in the field. "The early bird gets the worm", applies to pharmaceutical selling. We think leaving your house between 7:30 and 8:00 AM is a good rule. Starting later means you'll be playing catch up for the rest of the day.

☐ **Pre-Call.** Prepare for your first office call in your car. Your goal will be to introduce yourself to the physician, present a brief message on your product, meet the staff, and gather as much information on the office as you can in this first solo visit. Don't overdo it on your first call. Avoid using your first impression moment in a new office to present a cover to cover sales pitch to the physician. In those cases where you may not be able to see the physician, check with the receptionist to see if you can schedule an appointment with the doctor or maybe schedule a Lunch and Learn. But most, it is most important to learn the office protocol for reps in this first visit. You will no doubt be motivated to do it all once you're out of training, but just remember, it takes time. Pace yourself and stay focused on one or two goals per call for your first days. When you are finished and back in your car, take a few minutes to input what you've just learned into your computer. If you take time to do this now, it will pay off later. Keep things in perspective, *"Slow is smooth, and smooth is fast"*.

Week 1. You've made it through Week 1 on your own in the field! Now you have a well deserved weekend to get ready for next week. Here are a few tips to help you on a weekly basis.

☐ **Recap.** Never fail to do a recap of the day, making sure all your calls have been properly recorded in your database. Go over this again at the end of the week. This helps with making sure you're meeting your company "call goal".

- ☐ **Call Notes.** Review your notes for the week, especially in offices that were a first call. Ensure all names, addresses and office contact numbers are current in your database. Yes, this is tedious work, but invaluable in the beginning. Take the time up front to get it right! Get it right out of the chute, you'll keep the other reps back in the dust.

- ☐ **Route Changes.** Review you routing for the week and make adjustments designed to maximize the expense of time and effort. If you inherited an existing route, don't consider it carved in stone. There is probably a better, faster way. Take the extra step and find it.

- ☐ **Admin.** Meet all of your DM's weekly administrative requirements on time. Do not be late with your paperwork. This is always noted.

- ☐ **Communicate.** Check in with your District Manager at least once a week. You may need to contact your DM more frequently for other issues, but get into the habit of staying in touch with your DM weekly. Also, continue to talk regularly with your Field Trainer and counterparts, if any, on a regular basis. These people are a wealth of information. Remember, when in doubt, call someone.

Month 1. By now, you should have made at least one complete rotation in your territory. You are much more comfortable with your calls and have begun to develop a rapport with your physicians and the office. Not everything is going to happen in the first month, but some things will be getting better each week.

- ☐ **Voice Mail.** Send your success stories to your DM and your team mates. All reps need encouragement. Cohesiveness and team morale take off with these stories of success. Don't hesitate to send messages of encouragement to help your team. This will give you experience in communicating from the field to your DM and your team mates. Everyone will begin to know you're out there working hard.

- ☐ **Pre-Call.** Role-play in your car. Think through every scenario for each call before you enter the office. All the old timers do this, even after several years in the field.

- ☐ **Determination.** Never stop pushing yourself to be better. Strive for improvement every day. If things are not working out, ask yourself why. What can I do to make this better? Ask yourself this every day.

- ☐ **Staying Ahead.** Keep your eye on the goal; get to know your territory, your offices, the physicians and their staff by the end of your first three months.

Chapter Wrap. Your first day, week and month are the most challenging of your Career. Remember, it takes at least one quarter to begin to put it all together. It will come. Be patient and keep pushing yourself. Stick to the key points and you will be successful in your first month in the field. *"Slow is smooth and smooth is fast"*.

Chapter 3

Targeting, Routing and Sales Reports

As discussed in the previous chapter, planning is the key to success in Pharmaceutical Sales. Some key factors that will edge you from just a performer to a great one are effective targeting of your physicians, effective routing, call planning, and understanding your sales data. You showed up for training at the base level: essentially, here I am, train me to sell your product. Now, in your first month, you have by now worked your territory one complete cycle. Now it is time for the next level, to begin the transition from average sales rep to a really great sales rep.

Targeting. When you rode side-saddle with your field trainer, you started with a list of physicians in your territory, your physician target list, typically containing 100-125 physicians you will work with in your territory. On almost all target lists, each physician is ranked on the products that you sell. The scale runs from 1 to 10, with a 1 prescribing a large amount of your class of medicine to a 10, for a physician who prescribes little or none. Here are some key points to remember when organizing your target list:

- ☐ **Target Decile.** Organize your list by number, all 1thru 4's, 5's thru 7's, and 8's thru 10's. You can vary your groupings; just break the list into manageable sets of physicians based on the most sensible ranking. Remember, there will be far more targets in the middle and at the top of your list than at the bottom, sometimes simply because those physicians have been practicing medicine longer than other physicians in your territory.

- ☐ **Categorizing.** Break your list down further to show which physicians are the largest prescribers of your product in each group. (Be sure to include your products as well as your competitor's products.) This can be done with the data you have on the prescribing history for each of your physicians. It usually comes on an excel spreadsheet, making it easy to highlight the top prescribers in each category.

- ☐ **Current Business.** Then determine from the highlighted physicians in each group, which ones prescribe more of your product and which ones prescribe more of your competitor's products.

- ☐ **Strategy.** Develop a strategy. Your company may provide you with their own targeting plan to follow. In that situation, stick to the plan. Your company has invested time, money and effort to develop this plan, so set your company's call goals as your own. If not, the data you have pulled together now allows you to develop your own. Call on the physicians using your product in each group weekly. Start with the highest ranking and work down. These physicians are generating business now. You need to keep that on track. Next, begin calling on the physicians prescribing your competitor's products at about the same level. Find out why they favor the competing product over yours. Then develop a strategy to turn that around. Call on them weekly. Remember, your DM will always have the final say on strategy.

☐ **Opportunity.** Finally, for each category of your physicians one group will not be highlighted. These are your targets of opportunity. Call on them every other week until they start to prescribe your product. Then adjust you call plan as necessary. In the industry, this is sometimes referred to as, "low hanging fruit", meaning, they really are not prescribing much of any of the products for your class and with a little hard work, you can get them treating and prescribing.

Routing. (Territory Organization Plan-TOP) Establishing your route is a challenge for reps. Even after several years in the industry and working in territories that have been adjusted or realigned several times, seasoned reps still struggle with exactly how to set up their TOP. The best bet is to get to work on an 85% solution. Some territories are large, some small, some rural, some metropolitan. Whatever the case, your territory is yours and it is up to you alone to develop a TOP that meets your targeting strategy, meets your company's call plan objective, and drives market share, all at the same time. Several factors apply when organizing your TOP: access to the office, can I see the physician when I arrive at the office. What days are my key physicians in the office and can I see them on those days? Are there protocols in place for sales reps in the office? Here are some key points to remember.

- ☐ **2 Weeks.** Work toward a two week routing, though in some companies the standard may be a three or four week routing. Regardless of the size of the territory, a two week routing should be the goal. Keep in mind, though, that this will not happen at first. But after three months or so of working you should be approaching the 2 week goal.

- ☐ **Information Gathering.** Take the time up front to get all the information you need on when to call on the physicians. Start with the nurses or receptionists who are the gatekeepers. Write it all down, and then transfer it to your initial TOP as soon as you're in your car. If you call on a multi-physician clinic, and all of the physicians in that clinic are targets for you, you need to know the days and hours each of the physicians is in the office. Then annex each of the physicians individually. Some may be higher decile physicians than others. Get the information on all of the doctors and adjust your call plan for each practice accordingly.

- ☐ **Zones.** Break your territory into zones. You will need a map and the familiarity of your previous runs through your territory. For a large area you may need to operate in three or four zones; in smaller territories, you may need only two. This helps group your physicians by geography. Once your zones are established, you can determine which zone you will operate in on what day. All of this will be based on good intelligence work on all of your offices and making sure your efforts are economical in achieving your call plan.

Table 4: Setting Up Your Territory Organization Plan (TOP)

1. Export a list of all of your physicians in your database to an excel spreadsheet.

2. Make sure you add the physician rankings and all of the products you promote in the list. Then sort by city.

3. Cross-out any physicians you KNOW are no longer in your territory.

4. Cross-out any physician who has a specialty you do not call on.

5. Cross out any physician who has no ranking within your company product range.

6. Once you have completed steps one thru five, list the cities of your territory on a piece of paper, then from your target list, count the number of physicians you call on per city, and place that number next to the city listed on the paper.

7. Next, make a list of what cities could be worked on the same day. You should use the number of physicians per city, geography, driving distance to determine this. For example, if you have nineteen physicians in one city, it may not make sense to have that city combined with another city, bearing in mind, the industry standard of eight to ten physician calls per day.

8. Then use three blank TOP sheets to begin PENCILING in your TOP. First write the city or cities in the heading box below each day. Then pencil in the physicians that correspond with the city. You can go one step further if you know what days the physicians are in the office. Start with the total number of physicians divided by fifteen for a ballpark target for each day. Use your sheet with the number of targets per each city to determine this.

9. Next, use another blank TOP sheet to further refine what you have done from the first one. Use the first one to scratch, sort, and adjust physicians to another day etc. This is where all of the good field work you have done comes in to play for each of your offices. Remember, take the time now to get this right. It will pay off later. Pencil in your changes on the second blank sheet. Finally, take the third sheet and use this one as your final copy, the copy you will keep in your computer and your field binder.

10. Once you have completed your TOP, your next objective will be to follow it making adjustments as they occur.

11. Always look to your DM for advice and suggestions on your final TOP.

Table 5: Sample T.O.P

Week 1				
Monday	**Tuesday**	**Wednesday**	**Thursday**	**Friday**
Columbus	**Montgomery**	**Dothan**	**LaGrange**	**Auburn**
Physician	Physician	Clinic	Physician	Physician
Hospital	Physician	Physician	Physician	Hospital
Clinic	Clinic	Hospital	Physician	Physician

This is only a sample of what a TOP should look like. There may be several variations with every Pharmaceutical Company, Region, District and Territory. Bottom line, you need something like table 5, or a variation of it, to organize your day and maximize your time in your territory.

Sales Reports. This part of the reps job is the most demanding, yet, potentially the most rewarding. The purpose of this section is to help you to understand the different reports that are standard in the industry, and to emphasize the importance of setting aside the time to read and understand these reports. The sooner you master territory analysis, the better sales rep you will be. You can expect to see some variation of the following reports in the field.

- ☐ **The Weekly Report:** Not all companies may run this report; however, if you are fortunate to have it, take the time to understand it. The weekly report does not include all of the physicians in your database. Typically, it gathers prescribing data on the top 75-100 physicians in your territory, and is a snapshot of developments in your territory. These data can help you see trends in your territory, and whether or not your work in an office or city is paying off. These reports also report trends and activity with the competition. Remember, these reports are dated, usually two to three weeks behind.

- ☐ **The Monthly Report:** The same as the weekly report in format; however, the monthly report captures the prescription activity of all targeted physicians in your territory for an entire month. This report is critical to all reps in the field. It captures the business you have generated (or not generated) in the given month. Remember in pharmaceutical sales, **numbers do not lie.** The posting of monthly data is a time of stress or pride for reps, depending on how they are performing. If your numbers are trending down, you may have a difficult conversation with your DM; if your numbers are trending up; you are generally going to be given a little more autonomy.

- **Reading The Reports:** OK. You keep getting these excel spreadsheet reports with all of these numbers, all of my doctors, and, on top of all of the other things my DM has me doing, I am supposed to read and understand all of these reports. Sound familiar? You are not alone. All reps go through this and experience the stress of having too many tasks and not enough time. Welcome to the real world. Just focus yourself, and take the time to read and understand the reports. They will give you an understanding of your business, and increase your paycheck at the same time.

Start with your physicians and scroll through to see if they wrote any prescriptions of your product for the month. Usually this is presented as a percentage, so look at the competition as well. If there are four products in your therapeutic class, yours and three competitors, and Dr. Smith wrote 50% of your product in December, compare that 50% to the previous month to see if he went up or down. This can be a direct reflection of your effort if there was an increase, or a reflection of your lack of effort if there was a decrease. Keep in mind, this is where your District Manger can be of great help to you. Turn to your DM and ask for help in understanding the sales data.

Chapter Wrap. This chapter covers some of the most difficult tasks to master; however, if done correctly, it will determine your level of success. A point to remember: all of this takes time. One of the most difficult challenges in your first weeks in the field will be mustering the patience to master all your tasks. Repetition builds proficiency in all areas, and even after you have mastered your routing, your territory and your business, there is still room to grow. You will be stressed and pushed to the limit; however, if you work hard and have a positive attitude, it will fall into place.

Chapter 4

Why Should They See You: How To Distinguish Yourself From The Pack.

You are ready to go into your first large office, several doctors on your target list. They are large prescribers of your therapeutic area. You know you have your work cut out for you, you have done your pre-call planning, you have your action plan set; and now it is time to go in and start selling. Walking into the office, the first person you see is the receptionist. She has been multi-tasking since she arrived at 8am and has already seen several reps. You are smiling, cordial, and looking forward to getting back to see the physicians. The receptionist stops you in your tracks and informs you that the doctors are busy and are not being detailed this morning. They will, however, allow you to go back, drop off your samples in the sample closet, and get a signature from one of the doctors. You are happy to be going back to see the physicians and the office staff in the back; thank the receptionist and head to the sample closet.

With your samples correctly placed in your bin, you wait to speak to the physician about the benefits of your product over the competition. As the physician approaches, pulls a pen from his breast pocket and before you can say a word, he tells you he is backed up this morning and can only sign for the samples. He scribbles a signature and walks away, leaving you wondering if this is how every call will go in this particular office. This can be a typical sales call for some reps. But, you have the means to turn this around.

Just Another Sales Representative? How do you make an impact? How do you make a solid first impression? And how do you leave your mark from the first call in an office?

In virtually a sea of reps, what do you do to distinguish yourself? This chapter will focus on those factors that will keep you from being "just another sales representative".

- ☐ **Passion:** This is tag line. If you are not passionate about what you are doing, what and who you represent, and, critically, the impact your product will have on your patients, you will not break out of the pack. You have to believe in what you are doing. This is not a short lived venture. In some cases, you may be calling on some physicians for months before they agree to use your product. The passion can not fade; you must keep it going. Have a never quit attitude. Remember, many of the physicians you call on have been practicing medicine for years in the same practice. They have seen an army of reps come and go. It is up to you to convince them you are not just another rep.

- **Know Your Customers By Name:** This will make an immediate impact. Too many reps are interested only in the physicians, or those that impact the bottom line. Everyone in the office impacts the bottom line. Never overlook anyone in the practice. Learning the staff by name up front separates you from the pack. Most reps do not take the time to know all the staff by name; they focus only on the physicians, believing they are the ones that write the prescriptions. Don't make that mistake. Know the staff by name immediately, especially with your key customers.

- **110 Percent And Them Some:** What do you do for your customers within the guidelines of PhRMA Code on Interactions with Healthcare Professionals? Whatever it takes, is the short answer. These are the people who put food on your table and clothes on your back. If they ask, you deliver. Stay within PhRMA guidelines, your company's code of conduct and you will be fine. You'll send a clear message to the office that this rep means business. Immediate follow up is key, do not let too much time go by before getting back with the office on any issue.

- **Rule of 72:** It is a simple rule, but one always forgotten by the new reps. Never let more than 72 hours go by before following up on a request for action from an office. This may seem trivial, but your customers notice. If you always follow the rule, the office will soon know you mean business. If you can, try to get back within 24 hours. If the matter is urgent, get back immediately, within the same day. The office does not work for you, you work for them. This will be noticed.

- ☐ **The Golden Rule:** "Do unto others as you would have them do unto you", seems simple enough, but, it is sadly, often forgotten. The tales are legion where a rep was banned from an office. Don't let this happen to you. Some reps even take a perverse pride in having been banned from an office for confrontational selling. This is nonsense! Physicians are tight. Word will spread about a rude or pushy rep. Big town, small town, it will be the same result. There is a very fine line between challenging your customers in a sales call and being rude. Understand it and don't cross that line. You are a guest in your customer's office, just as you would be a guest in their home.

- ☐ **Dress For Success:** This is no cliché. It makes a difference. If you look professional, you feel professional, and you will be professional. When you go into an office for a sales call, you need to show that confidence. Your customers will see it and they'll remember you. But, there is a fine line. You need to follow – don't overdo it and don't underdo it. Look professional. For men that means a business suit with coat and tie; for women, a business suit with a jacket. When male representatives walk into an office with just shirt and tie and no jacket, they look unprofessional. Females can also make mistakes with skirts too short or blouses to tight. This is common sense in the professional world.

Chapter Wrap. Your company can train you on your product. It can focus you on the ways to sell your product. It can position your product over your competition. But you are the only one who can put those things together in the field. Keeping your focus, maintaining the passion for what you do will make the difference. You must know your customers and build strong, lasting relationships with them. This can only be done by building trust. When your offices know you believe in what you are doing and are passionate about your product it radiates outward and separates you from the pack.

Chapter 5

Field Rides With Your District Manager

You will have to prepare for field rides with your District Manager (DM). This is a source of stress for some, but an opportunity for all to show your DM the hard work you have been doing to grow your business and build your customer relationships. Most training departments do not spend much time on field rides; their focus has been preparing you to sell their product. Knowing something about what to expect, however, can be a big help. Remember, you only have one shot at a first impression with your DM. This chapter will outline some of the steps necessary to make it a good one.

How to prepare and what to expect: Most DM's in the industry will let their reps know in advance that they are dropping in for a field ride. There are several steps you should take in preparation for this event. But first, understand what it really is.

In the military, one of the methods used to gauge readiness is to conduct an inspection. If you treat it like a military inspection, you'll be about right. Your field ride is no different; it is an inspection of how you're handling your territory, and how you're doing your job. This chapter will focus on some tips to prepare you and to make your field ride successful.

- ☐ **Types of Field Rides:** On average, your DM will ride with you once every four to six weeks. Field rides are usually 1-2 days long, and are conducted in your territory as you are calling on your customers. One day field rides are common when there is a new DM assigned or for about six months after your company launches a new product. Otherwise, your field rides will usually be two days. The first day will focus on making calls on your customers and doing an evaluation of each call as you work through the day. The second day will focus on some calls in the morning, with the afternoon spent on reviewing the field ride and focusing on any issues your DM feels are important. This is your time to shine. Plan ahead and execute.

- ☐ **Preparing for the Field Ride:** Many DM's will have standard reports to capture all of a field ride. Get the forms that will be used and complete them in advance. The forms will have data on your territory, where you will be on each day of the field ride, the customers you will call on, along with their current prescribing data. Your DM will also know your current market share, your current ranking in the district, region and nation, plus any number of other facts on your performance. Remember, your DM has been around a while, and has personally demonstrated success in the field. Do not try to stack the deck by filling your day with your best customers. Keep your routing the same as it would be if your DM was not riding with you. You might talk to some of your more tenured district teammates about what to expect if you have any questions. Remember, prior planning prevents poor performance. And don't try to game your DM, he or she has been there before!

- [ ] **Territory Binders:** Most companies require each rep to keep a daily territory binder while in the field. The binder contains all the information you need to run your territory, and it gives your DM a quick reference to assess your proficiency. For every field ride make sure your territory binder is up to date, in the right format, and ready to hand to your DM.

- [ ] **Your Car, Trunk and Storage Area:** A Pharmaceutical Sales Rep does not have the typical office. Our business is conducted out of our home office, our car and our storage area (if we have samples). Some DM's may want to see your home office when they drop in for a field ride; however, most will simply ride "side-saddle" with you for the day. Your car, then, is your office. When your DM pitches up, consider it an inspection. You will spend most of your time in the car with your DM, so make a good showing. Make sure your car is clean, make sure your trunk is organized with your patient education information items, and just remember that everything, including how you maintain your car, will be evaluated. Some reps with messy disorganized cars have been told by their DM's to take them back to their hotel, and come back when the car was clean and the trunk was organized. How's that for a first impression.

Another area that may be inspected during your field day visit by your DM is your storage area. If you have samples, chances are you have a storage area to hold them as well as your patient education items. Like your car, make sure your storage area is neat and organized. Make sure all of the boxes are open with the box top flaps cut off with a utility knife. This allows for better viewing of box contents and avoids the scene of boxes that have never been opened and a mess that declares that you have no idea what is there. Take care of your car and your storage area. There won't be a chance for a second impression.

Table 6: Sample Field Day Itinerary

Representative Name:

Prepared For: DM

Date/s:

Day 1 and Day 2

Physician Name	Sales Aids Used	Physician Decile	Product 1	Product 2	Call Objective

Table 7: Sample Contents For Territory Binder

1. Territory Map
2. Territory TOP / Routing
3. Territory Business Plan
4. Current Monthly / Weekly Data
5. Managed Care Plans and Information
6. Clinical Studies For Your Products
7. Calendar For Next 3 Months Printed
8. Phone Roster For District and Region

Table 8: Sample Trunk Diagram

Shoe Bag w/divider for smaller items

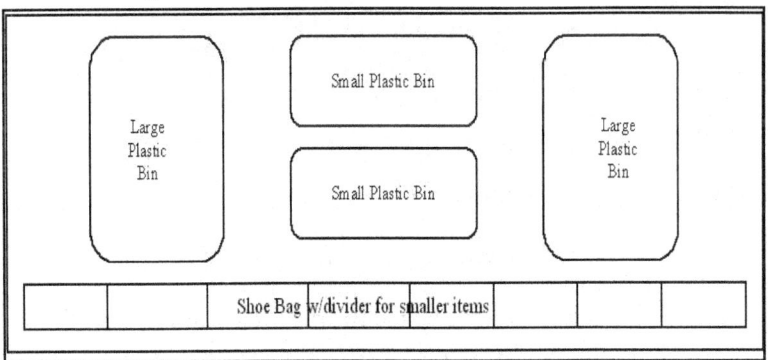

Rear Bumper

☐ **The Night Before:** Most DM's will ask you when and where you want to meet. This is probably a test, though your DM may not admit it. Field Ride meeting times should be between

7:30 and 8:00 AM. Getting an early start allows you more time with your manager. Remember, this is a positive opportunity for you. You won't have all that many chances to interact with your DM, so take advantage of the limited time that you have. Arrange the meeting time a couple of days in advance, and confirm it the night before. Here is a checklist to help you plan your first ride:

- Car washed, trunk organized, samples stored correctly
- Storage area clean, organized, presentable and accessible
- Day 1 and Day 2 itinerary filled out (make 2 copies)
- Know your routing each day and have that mapped out on paper
- Gas tank full and all FLEET papers in order
- Territory Binder is current
- All lunches coordinated with catering company the day before
- Passenger seat empty for DM
- Reserve space in the back seat of car for DM's coat and computer bag
- Make sure your car is completely packed and ready to go the night before; do not leave anything for the morning
- Have an umbrella large enough for 2 people

- Get a good nights sleep
- Have a backup alarm
- <u>Do not be late</u>. Leave an hour early if necessary. If the DM is late, that is on him/her. The rep, you must always be on time, or better yet, fifteen minutes early

☐ **Day 1:** Field rides are a source of anxiety for some reps and a pleasant experience for others. With effective planning and execution of the two day process, you will be in the latter group. If you have followed the steps outlined above, you are ready to go. Then relax. If you have been doing your job, you'll have nothing to worry about.

When you start your ride, hand the DM the itinerary. Be prepared to discuss any issues that the DM may have concerning your territory, and when you arrive at each office, be prepared to discuss your pre-call planning for that office, including your call objective for the office. Do not expect to move at your usual pace when your DM is with you. Plan to run at about 75% of your normal rate because of pre and post call discussions with your DM. Some reps get a little too focused on trying to achieve call plan on every field ride. Remember, DM's are coaches; they are watching over you with a world experience as their backdrop. They will see things in one call that you may not have seen in the last ten calls in an office. Pay attention to and learn from your DM.

☐ **Day 2:** The second day of a field ride is time for you to apply the things you learned on the first day. The typical day 2 morning will involve making some calls and applying the lessons learned the first day. This is the moment to show improvement! The afternoon will be reserved for a sit down with your DM to review your progress, your future development and other issues your territory. Make sure to have your list of things to discuss with your DM. This is your opportunity to let your DM know what you think. Take advantage of it. Finally, your DM will use this session to go over your two day field ride and have you sign your report.

- **The Company Car:** Your company will provide you with a company car, fuel card, maintenance schedule and allow limited personal use for a small monthly charge. Your company owns this vehicle and is loaning it to you so you can do your job. In some cases upon being hired, you may be given the outgoing territory reps company vehicle as a start. Every two years thereafter or depending on the mileage, your FLEET Service will send you order information on your new car. This consists of a list of eligible vehicles in the make and model you choose. It is your job to maintain your company car by following the maintenance schedule, to include making sure the correct air pressure is in the tires and it is clean both inside and out. Your manager will inspect your company car when he rides with you in the field. DM's notice immediately if your company car is dirty and poorly kept. This is a direct reflection on you and will be noted. Your company car is your office on wheels, where you spend the majority of your day, so take care of it. Clean and organized will always beat lots of clutter. Your company will allow you a moderate car wash every few weeks, so, there is no excuse in not keeping your car clean and maintained. Your car should be a source of pride, which in turn becomes an extension of how you run your territory.

Chapter Wrap. Field Rides with your DM are a necessary and integral part of this industry. All companies go through a painstaking process in selecting their field reps. Being selected as a field rep means your company has placed its trust in you. Pay back that trust by being prepared when your DM sends you the message alerting you to an upcoming 2 day field ride. Follow the steps outlined in the chapter and you will have a successful ride.

Chapter 6

Meetings: District, Region, National And Other

Pharmaceutical Sales Representatives attend meetings throughout the year, a necessity in such a decentralized industry. Reps work each day in their territories, communicate by phone, email or company voice mail, but can go weeks without seeing any of their teammates face-to-face. There is constant change within any pharmaceutical company, and, it will be necessary to gather the sales force for periodic meetings to help them buy into the changes. This chapter discusses some of the meetings reps will attend each year, how to prepare for them, protocol tips, travel tips and, in general, how to make it through these meetings. One key thing to remember: you'll get out of the meetings what you put into them. Attitude is everything, especially during sales meetings. Absorb these tips and you will shine at all your company sales meetings

Types of Meetings. We already covered your training meetings in the previous chapter. These meetings focus on keeping the sales force tuned up, updated on current/new products, new indications of existing products or a new product launch meeting. The purpose of this is to make sure you know which meetings you as a sales representative will typically see and what to do to prepare for those meetings.

- ☐ **District Meetings:** The District Meeting will be the most common for reps, and easiest to manage. It is arranged at the district manager level; and the logistics and cost of gathering everyone in the district for one or two days are less cumbersome, than the larger Regional or National Meetings. The district meeting is typically one or two days long, normally starting on a Tuesday and ending on a Wednesday. Your district manager will set the agenda, and forward to you the information you must complete before attending. Here are some tips that will make you stand above your teammates.

  - **Do not be late:** Don't cut it too close. If necessary, ask your DM for permission to arrive the night before. Then all you have to do is get up and go downstairs to the meeting.

  - **Come prepared to work and prepared to participate:** Your DM had a reason for sending all of that pre-work for you to complete before the meeting. More often than not, the District Managers have come fresh from a District Managers Meeting, and the information the DM's received from Corporate Headquarters is now being pushed down to the sales force at the district meeting. Your DM did not just grab all of this new information out of the air; there is a reason for all of it. Do your pre-work and show up prepared and ready to participate.

- **Be an active team member:** The company is spending time and money to bring your district reps together. The least you can do is to be energetically engaged during the meeting. Your participation will be measured against that of your peers. Your manager will immediately see that you came prepared, and that you have an interest in the business and the direction of the company. There will be sales reps whose behavior will make one wonder why they even showed up at all. They might look unhappy, perhaps complaining about why they can't seem to make it into the winners circle, or why their bonus was so low. It will always be someone else's fault. Don't be part of that group. Set yourself apart. Be active.

- **Volunteer:** A tremendous amount of work goes into preparing for a district meeting. One thing you can do to help with the DM's workload is volunteer to take the lead on one of the tasks for the meeting. This could mean preparing handouts, doing some research on a clinical trial and presenting it to the district, or actually leading a session during the meeting. You could volunteer to help set up a meeting room, or bring in some things to help support the meeting. Regardless of your position in the sales force or district, there is always something you can do to volunteer to help make the meeting more productive. This is not apple polishing; it's team building!

- **Protocol and etiquette:** District meetings bring out the good, the bad and the ugly in the district's business. Often enough, it is a negative experience for some, particularly if their territory is not doing well. DM's will recognize and award the top performers and take note of the laggards. Remember, as we stated in the earlier chapters, everything reps do in the field is tracked and tabulated. Performance is reducible to numbers on growth or decline charts. And numbers do not lie. Against that reality, there is opportunity for top performers to shine at district meetings and an equal opportunity for others to see there is work to do in their territory. So, what do you do if you find your self at the top, in the middle or on the bottom, (bearing in mind, if you are reading this manual then you are shooting for the top, and might be on your way there in short order.) Here are some tips that will make you stand out as you interact with your teammates at the meetings:

    1. If you are on top or ranked #1, be gracious. Do not boast about it; rather share the best practices of your success with your district.

    2. Do not always be the first one to speak up. It is fine once or twice, but

hold back a little. Let others open up and then bring yourself into the conversation.

3. If a teammate is doing something well, offer congratulations. Ask for tips on how they are getting their results.

4. When others talk, use active listening techniques to stay with the conversation.

5. Stay for the entire meeting, especially when your teammates are running a session. (No computers open, no newspaper reading, no text messaging, no distracting sidebar conversations).

6. Do not hold back on ways to improve business. But be tactful when doing so. Avoid "dime dropping" or "call outs" of your teammates.

7. Don't create cliques in the district. Get to know all of your teammates.

☐ **Region Meetings.** Region level meetings are less frequent than district meetings, because of the costs and the logistics involved in bringing an entire region together. There are different configurations for pharmaceutical companies; however, most are composed of between four and eight Regions across the United States. Each Region may consist of from five to ten Districts. On average, you could have between fifty to a hundred Sales Representatives in one Region. This explains why there are only a few Region meetings during a year. Typically, region meetings are usually one or two days longer than district meetings. The parameters we mentioned for the district meetings apply for the region meetings, and there will always be time allocated for DM's to conduct district business at these meetings. But, there are some differences between District and Region level meetings, so follow these tips for the region meetings and make your mark just as you did at the district meeting:

- Region meetings involve crowds of people. Don't get lost in the crowd.

- Even though daily events may seem more chaotic than at the district meetings, the same rules apply. Don't be late. Always know when and where you are supposed to be.

- Many of the sessions at Region Meetings are conducted at the Region level with everyone in one room. Do not let that stop you from getting involved or sharing your experiences from the field with others. Volunteer. Don't be afraid to add your comments to a discussion.

- Region Meetings usually include some after business day activities, such as a district dinner or an awards banquet. The ironclad rule is: never do anything to embarrass your district. If you have questions about protocol issues, talk to some of your more tenured teammates.

- Be aware of your surroundings, and always assume that you are "on display". Region meetings will attract the senior leadership in the company. Be careful what you say, even to a teammate. You never know who else might be listening. In that same channel, if you are conversing with someone you do not know, be careful what you say, you could be talking to the CEO of the company.

☐ **National Meetings:** These meetings are the end all of the meetings for the year, and are usually held in January. A second national meeting in one year might involve the launch of a new drug. National Meetings will always be a week long, beginning on Monday and ending at noon on Friday to allow for travel. In many cases, your company may select Sunday as the initial travel day to the meeting site. National Meetings are huge logistical operations and Pharmaceutical Companies will hire outside agencies to develop and run the meetings. You can expect to stay at a top notch hotel/resort with days packed from 8 AM to 6 PM, followed by a company driven event until 9 or 10 PM. Though the dynamics of National Meetings can be overwhelming, the parameters for District and Region Meetings still apply. If you follow the rules for those meetings, you will be fine. With that said, national meetings are still different, because of their sheer size. So here are a few tips for navigating through a national meeting:

- National Meetings involve hundreds or even thousands of people from your company; the entire company is at one location. Expect long lines at every event. Show up early, including for meals.

- Know where your district teammates are at all times. Stay in touch with them, and if possible try to sit together. It is fine to visit with the friends you trained with at national meetings, but, don't distance yourself from your district. Stay together as a team at National Meetings.

- When the entire company is taking part in an activity, and there is an opportunity to speak or ask a question, make sure you have your thoughts well organized before you speak into the microphone. Never be discouraged from being active, volunteering or getting involved, but when you are on a national stage, the impression you make will be seen through a looking glass. If your comfort level for speaking out is the district or region meeting, stay there for a while. Don't use a national meeting to step outside your comfort zone unless you are very confident in what your are going to say or ask.

- Stay out of trouble. National Meetings have a way of bringing the best or worst out in some people, especially after all of the business of the day is done. The following quote from a former DM in the industry keeps things in perspective, " *Nothing good happens after midnight at a National Meeting*". If you want to unwind with some friends in the lounge for a few minutes, fine, but get to bed by 11:00-11:30 PM. Don't close the bar down every night. You could embarrass yourself and your district.

Chapter Wrap: Meetings are a big part of the Pharmaceutical Industry. How you prepare and conduct yourself at each meeting can set you apart from your peers. If you plan for a long career in this or any industry, it is important to start out right, get your feet on the ground, set a good impression, gain the respect of your peers and the positive attention of your management. Follow the simple tips we have outlined in this chapter and you will be on your way to impressing all of those around as well a setting yourself up for a promising career in this unique industry.

Chapter 7

The Call: 30 Second Detail To Full Presentation, "How to do this in the real world".

This is the bread and butter of Pharmaceutical Sales, putting your field craft to work with your customers. This chapter will focus on what happens out in the field, not review what you learned in training. It will focus on when you should make a full presentation call to a physician, or when you should just make the key points and move on. In training, reps are taught to go cover to cover with the physicians. This is a good technique for training, but, in real life situations, knowing when to go cover to cover and when not to on your first calls can affect your longer term future performances. There are many factors that dictate how the call will go. We will explore these in this chapter, emphasizing what works in the field and what does not.

Types Of Calls: The key to understanding how far to go with the physician is first understanding the different types of calls you will use in the field. With that understanding, you will learn which way to go based on the situation in the office when you first walk through the door.

- ☐ **The Full Presentation Call:** Also known as "going cover to cover." This call works just great for role plays in training, when the five minute time clock is running. And it is a necessary practice. However, this will not be your typical call. It is important to understand the practice of going cover to cover, but don't expect it to be the norm. In the following situations you may have this type of call:

  - **Lunch And Learn:** When you bring lunch in for the office, it offers a good opportunity to share more information with the physicians. There will be more time allocated with the physicians and most will understand that you will be making a longer presentation.

  - **A New Product:** When a new product is launched, there is a good opportunity to share more information with the physicians either in a stand-up call or a Lunch and Learn. Most physicians will be interested in hearing about a new product, particularly if it is a new therapeutic class of medicine, as opposed to a new product in an already crowded class of medicine. But remember, you won't be able to ride the new product wave for more than one shot for a full presentation. So make the best of it.

- **A New Clinical Trial:** This important information is for all physicians; with emphasis on those who studied clinical data in medical school. Most are interested in new studies and clinical trials. But again, you'll probably only have one shot per physician.

- **A New Indication:** Similar to a new product launch, using the new indication information for a full presentation on your customers is acceptable.

- **Your First Sales Call:** Try not to use your first call for a full presentation. If you are calling on an office for the first time, the staff and the physicians are more likely to give you a little extra time to introduce yourself and identify your product. Use the time to establish a good first impression. Sell yourself first!

- **The Busy Office:** The moment you walk into the office, you must be able to pick up on the atmosphere and make a determination of how the call should go. If the physicians are swamped, (a packed waiting room), do not try for a full presentation. You'll only leave a negative lasting impression with the physician and the staff.

- **When The Office Protocol Prohibits Full Presentation Details:** Every office has a protocol for reps. Know what it is and do not violate it. If the office protocol does not allow full presentations, don't attempt to do one. You'll only leave a negative lasting impression and won't be getting much business from this customer.

- ☐ **The One – Two Minute Call:** This type of call is more the norm; however, it also has its limitations as well. In this call, you will present key information to position your product with the competition. It requires important pre-call planning, since you're targeting a specific area of the competition. The best representatives, the ones with the best relationships with their customers will have this kind of call down to an art. Their calls flow naturally, and they always seem to get time with the physicians. This does not happen automatically. It takes time and practice. Remember, pre-call planning will always make every call more effective.

- ☐ **The 30 Second Call:** This is the call you will use most frequently. Understand this, the medical community is overwhelmed. Physicians and staff are overworked and offices are understaffed, yet the number of patients coming in to the office continues to rise. With that formula, it is easy to see why physician offices will have stringent protocols for reps. Add to that the number of reps advocating the same product and same message calling on the office several times a week and it should be easy to understand why offices are pushing back with strict protocols for reps. With that in mind, the 30 second call requires meticulous planning, a clear understanding of the competition, and prescribing trends for the office. Additionally it requires a well rehearsed plan to get your message across in a short time with enough effectiveness to convince the physician to use your product over that of the competition. Realistically, you can plan for the one to two minute call, but will most likely deliver a thirty second call to the physician. Make the most of it.

☐ **The Signature Only Call:** This call is commonly used in offices with no access to the physicians except for a Lunch and Learn. In this call, the front office staff ask you what samples you have and check to see if they need any. If they do, the receptionist will ask you to send your computer or signature pad back and allow you to stand in a designated spot so you can view the physician signing for the samples. This designated spot is usually far enough away from the physician so you can not detail him/her but meets the guidelines outlined for delivering samples to an office. Unfortunately, many of the physicians that you must see are in offices that have such protocols because they are so busy.

Overcoming Obstacles To The Call: We have discussed the different types of calls. Now for some of the small details you can use to help you make sound decisions that will gain you favor on future calls. You learned in training to present your message to the physician, get them to agree with your key points, close for more or continued use of your product, and do this in a full detail presentation. Again, this is great for training, but the field environment doesn't always work out this way. The industry has changed over the past several years, and continues to change. Some offices have completely banned reps, and some have banned the delivering of samples of any kind. You must understand that you were not hired to complain about the situation; you were hired to get out there and grow your business. Just as in the military, if you encounter an obstacle, go around it, under it, over it or right through the middle of it. The important thing is to find a way to overcome the obstacle. Here are some tips you can use to overcome obstacles and change that "signature only" or "30 second call" into a one – two minute call, and a one – two minute call into a full presentation every time you visit an office.

- ☐ **Scan The Parking Lot:** If you drive into the parking lot of an office and see that it is full, make adjustments to your plan. Full means the office may be backed up with patients and the physician may not be seeing many reps that day. An empty parking lot may be a sign that things are not too busy and you may have more time that day. In either case, make a mental note and move forward with your plan. If you encounter another rep in the parking lot who has already been to the office, find out which physicians are in that day, and what the situation is inside. Regardless of your "assessment" of the parking lot, make a call.

- ☐ **Scan The Waiting Room:** The first thing you should always do when you walk into the office is scan the waiting room. This is for a couple of reasons: first to gauge the crowd, second to see if there are other reps waiting to go back and see the physician. If the waiting room is full and there is another rep waiting, you may want to adjust the plan. If the room is empty or only has a few patients, you may want to make an adjustment to your plan, and try for more time.

Regardless of the waiting room situation, go to the receptionist window and find out which physicians are in and if you can go back.

☐ **Check In With The Receptionist:** The front office receptionist is one of the most important people a rep will deal with. She (usually) is the gatekeeper of the office and has the absolute power to help you or hinder you. In very busy offices such as multi-physician clinics, this position is often very stressful. In addition to dealing with sick patients all day long, receptionists also have to manage the reps. You want this person on your side. Here are some tips that may help.

- Get to know them by name

- Ask them how their day is going

- Find out the pace of the office for that day

- Ask what kind of mood the physicians are in and which physicians are in the office that day

- Find out which physician/s were on call the night before (this will tell you immediately the kind of mood the physician will be in for the day)

- If you are calling on the office for the first time, find out what the office protocol for Sales Reps is at this time

- If the office has an lunch or appointment system, always take the time to schedule a follow up appointment before you leave the office.

- Always check out with the front office staff and thank them for their help.

☐ **Check In With The Physician's Nurse:** Once you get into the back office, check in with the nurse to see how things are going. Never assume that just because the waiting room is full and the office has seen many patients that day, that you will not have an opportunity to speak with the physician. Many physicians are used to this busy schedule, and do not mind talking to reps. As you learn to work with each of your offices and develop good relationships, your calls will improve. Remember, if the nurse tells you the physician is very busy and only has time to sign for samples, respect that. Do not violate the rules. You may feel good by squeezing out some extra time with the physician, but you might do it at the cost of jeopardizing your relationship with the nurse. That could blow back on your next call.

☐ **Read Body Language:** One of the biggest mistakes reps make is failing to read the body language of the office or staff. Often we are so focused on our task and objective that we fail to see these important things around us. One of the trademarks of a successful reps is the ability to read body language and understand the non-verbal ques. Take the time to invest in books on Non-Verbal Communication, Interpersonal-Communication or Effective Listening. You can also look into any online courses your company may have on these topics.

These are just some of the tools that can help in extending the call and getting you a little more time with the physician. The most important thing to remember in striving to get more time with physicians in this changing environment is to not give up. Finding ways to navigate through the obstacles so you can spend the time you need with the physician, develop relationships with the staff and sell your product over your competition.

Chapter Wrap: The key to success in Pharmaceutical Sales today is getting more quality time with your physicians in an environment that works against that goal. Having a can do attitude, the persistence to never give up, and the ability to find ways to overcome obstacles will separate you from the pack. In the history of sales, there have been very few products where the rep sits at the home office desk and takes calls from offices asking when you are coming to them. Being a successful rep takes work, determination and the ability to adapt and overcome.

Chapter 8

Going The Extra Mile

"Going the extra mile" is a phrase that you hear several times from the senior leadership in your company. When you are at your next sales meeting or awards ceremony for your district or region, ask yourself, "why is it that the same people are awarded again and again, year after year"? Did they go through a different training course? Did they get special attention? The answer is no, they did not. They went through the same training as you, and they have the same struggles and difficulties that every rep faces in the field. So what makes them so different? Perhaps they have learned to go the extra mile every day. In this chapter we will discuss different ways the average rep can go the extra mile to improve sales, develop customer relationships and peer relationships, and ultimately, repeatedly end up in the winners circle.

How Can I Get Better: As Pharmaceutical Sales Representatives you can slip into a rut from time to time. Your sales might be flat, or you may have worked your territory for so long that you believe it has reached its peak potential in sales growth. You may well believe that the relationships you have built over the years with certain physicians are just fine. But are they good enough to get more growth. If these thoughts run through your mind while you are driving or taking a mental time out to think about your business, then it is time for you to think about going the extra mile. For many reps, managing "the rut" is the difference between a record year and a static year. An average rep can end up in the winners circle by fluke, by falling into a good situation and letting it carry for a year; however, the rep that is a winner two years in a row or more over a sales career is never average. These winning reps are different. If you want to be a winner, then lets dig in and look at some ways to go the extra mile.

- ☐ **It Always Starts With Attitude:** "Attitude is everything" applies to pharmaceutical sales. Your attitude for the day starts the moment your feet hit the ground. Taking that a step further, it begins with the time you set your alarm to launch your day. If you're rolling out of bed at 7:30 or 8:00 AM, and begin making your first office calls at 9:00 AM, you're already behind both mentally and physically. Make a change. Get out of the house and be on the road to your first office by 8:00 to 8:30. In our industry, your home office is not your environment; that is in the field. So get to work early in your territory.

- ☐ **Plan And Prepare:** "Prior planning prevents poor performance" did not come from thin air. Those who take the extra time to plan and prepare their day in pharmaceutical sales always have a much better understanding of their business. It is no surprise that they are also the most successful. With that in mind, here are some tips for success.

- **Develop A Daily Personal Reminder:**
  Every rep needs a daily reminder. Perhaps this is one you could use, "I am directly responsible for everything that happens in my territory", or perhaps this one, "if I do not give 110% and then some every day, my sales will be low, my territory will fail and I may lose my job". Recite your reminder in front of the mirror, or print it out and place it in your company car. Read it every day as a reminder.

- **Plan For Your Day The Night Before:**
  What do you do when you get home at the end of the day. If you put all your business related items on your desk and leave them there until you leave the next day, chances are you won't have a plan going into each day. This is not to say you need to work around the clock. But, you will have to put in some extra time at the end of the day to make sure you are re-loaded for the next day. Develop a system to manage all of the things that developed while you were in the field that day. Remember, most companies require you to log all of your calls daily, and log onto the company network so all of the data can be tabulated. In addition, you may have requirements from your DM, emails to answer, or any additional duties that you have within the district to work on. You must take the time to look at your calendar

and plan your next day, reload your car with items for offices and make sure you have your routing down. Finally, print out your TOP and pencil in any adjustments that you need to make for the next day.

- **Go To Bed Early / Get Up Early:** If you stay up every night until midnight, you will be dragging by the time you hit Wednesday, and your productivity will drop. Your customers will see you looking tired and worn down, and that has consequences. Set a time for yourself each night and stick to it, try to shoot for 10 PM and definitely no later than 10:30 or 11 PM to call it a day. Remember, shoot for a daily goal of being on the road between 7:30 and 8:00 AM.

- **Plan For 30 Minutes to 1 Hour of Exercise Daily:** It is critically important to keep yourself physically fit. Try to plan for at least half an hour of exercise in your day. This does not have to be first thing in the morning; it can be later in the afternoon after you are done with your calls. It will help you decompress and clear your mind for the next day. This is a high stress job; exercise can keep that stress in check.

- **Conduct A Daily Personal Assessment Of Yourself:** At the end of the day, when you are driving home, turn off the radio and reflect on what you accomplished in your day. Did you sell? Did you move share for your company? Were the calls you made today effective? Did they leave a lasting impression on your customer? If you had any situations that did not go as planned, ask yourself how will I improve next time. Take a few minutes to think about how you might be better tomorrow. Do not be one of those reps who throws everything in the back seat of the car, and simply zones out with the radio blasting on the way home. Take time to reflect in the quiet of your field office, your car.

- **Do Something Each Week To Improve Yourself Personally/Professionally:** Ask yourself, at the end of each week, what did I do to improve myself personally and professionally this week. If the answer eludes you, then you need to do some thinking. It might be as simple as getting a new pair of dress shoes or new business attire. Polishing your shoes, doing an online course that your company provides to improve yourself developmentally, getting your company car cleaned, washed and maintenanced, updating your field binders, just about anything. When the weekend comes around, do not check out until Monday morning. Stay focused. Don't get locked into the idea that your weekends are completely off. No American industry works that way.

☐ **Flawless Execution:** The sales call and customer relationships are the essence of pharmaceutical sales. It takes time, but if you follow the pointers outlined in this chapter, your market share will grow, your relationships with your customers will solidify, and you will end up in the winners circle at the end of the year. Follow these tips for increased success.

- **What Are The Needs Of Your Customers:** As reps we are trained to get into the office, present our call and close for business. Similarly, our physicians have become conditioned to receive our quick message, sign and walk away. We must modify that paradigm. One way to do this is to find out what your customers need, what you can do to make their life easier. Is there any resource at your disposal to add value to the office. Some companies offer medical textbook programs for physicians or have opportunities to allow physicians to act as speakers at medical seminars. Some companies have separate divisions that will allow a representative to come to an office and provide updated education to the staff on reimbursement changes at no charge to the office. So, how does this apply to the rep in the field? Simple. Know the resources available in your company. Do the research. Ask the questions. Find out everything you can about every resource and use those resources again to take care of your customers. Offices will always remember the reps who bring value, who make life just a little easier.

- **Take Notes and Follow Up Immediately:** You can enhance your relationships with your customers by just pulling out a notepad or a business card to take notes on any issue that the office or physician may think important. This small step builds credibility. It shows you are listening, are tuned in and are going to take action. Have your notepad and pen ready, and remember the, *"Rule of 72"*, with emphasis on getting back with an answer within 72 hours or sooner.

- **Don't Forget Your Customers:** One of the traps reps fall into is to "forget" their customers once they become loyal supporters. Don't get lulled into thinking once you have a loyal customer using your product, it is automatic. If anything, maintaining that loyalty is the challenge. Remember, your competition gets paid just as much as you do to draw your loyal customers away from you. Getting a new customer using your product over the competition may be the easy part; keeping them loyal to your product in the face of daily competition is the challenge. Don't let your loyal customers see a change in the way they are treated once they are fully committed and using your product. Your frequency of calls, and willingness to meet new needs of the loyal customer should never change. One final rule; never assume anything; always stay on top of what is happening with your loyal customers; your competition is out there.

- **Think Outside The Box:** We have all heard this before, but as a rep in the field, it doesn't take long before you may find yourself not making the progress you had planned with your customers. If this happens, challenge yourself with ideas outside your normal pattern. If the only way to see a physician is to schedule end of the day appointments at 5PM, schedule as many as you can. If you call on a no access office, invite the physicians to attend educational, speaker sponsored health care professional dinner programs. If you hear that one of your key physicians is attending a large medical convention that your company supports, volunteer to work your exhibit booth at the convention. If you can not see any of the physicians at the office, find out if there is a way to sponsor one of the Grand Rounds Sessions at the hospital with one of your speakers. You get the idea. Never be satisfied with the status quo; never let an obstacle stop you; constantly challenge yourself with new ideas.

Chapter Wrap: Going the extra mile will separate you from the pack. This chapter is designed to give you some of the tools and ideas to do so. However, as we stated in the beginning of this chapter, it all starts with attitude. If you do not have the fire and the passion when you hit the field each day, then perhaps it is time for you to reflect on what or where you want to be within your company. You are in this business because you are an achiever, you love challenges and want to be the best. You hold all of the keys and tools to be successful. The question is, do you have the PASSION and energy to go the extra mile.

Chapter 9

Surviving In A Changing Environment

The Pharmaceutical Industry has been in a state of almost constant change in recent years. In the closing years of the last century, the large pharmaceutical companies had good medicines in the early years of their patent life cycle. Exciting times, with plenty of competition, plenty of products that were already available or ready for launch pending FDA approval. Fast forward to 2008/2009, chronicle the changes, all of them inevitable. Some companies adjusted well to change; others did not. Though no one can predict the future for the industry, the smart money will bet on change, almost constant wrenching change. Accept it as part of the industry environment. As the companies make adjustments, and position themselves for the future, move their pipeline of products through FDA approval, and contend with their "gold standard" products going generic, your own survival in this amazing industry will be solely up to you. Let's explore some ways you can be a survivor and keep moving ahead.

How Can I Survive All Of This Change: If you have been in the industry for five years or more, you have experienced multiple redeployments or realignments of the sales force. These terms are synonymous with Pharmaceutical Sales. Your challenge is to keep your job in the face of company reorganization almost every year. Company reorganizations or outright mergers are predictable to an extent; how you survive, and how you keep your sanity during times of change will be up to you. Let's look at some ways you can make it through these difficult times and come out better and stronger.

- ☐ **Bet On Change:** Many of the blockbuster drugs of the 1990's are open to generic competition. This will continue over the next few years. Many companies bulked up their sales forces to drive those aging products, and now those same companies must design a sales force for the current environment in the face of even stiffer competition. Company announcements of sales force reduction of ten to twenty percent are common. So, how does the rep in the field deal with this instability.

    - **Keep Your Focus:** You can only control what is yours: your business, your territory, your customers and your market share growth. Regardless of what senior management is planning, nothing changes the fact that you still have a job and business to run. Stay in touch with your DM, and keep working every day.

    - **Stay Away From The Rumor Mill:** If you think there is really something going on that affects you, call your DM and get it straight. Don't get caught up in the rumor mill; it takes you off of the target and keeps you off balance.

- **Stay Put:** Some reps today will bolt a company at the first hint of a sales force reorganization. There is a real danger in that. Many companies outsource their reorganization. What this means is that an outside agency will survey the sales force and determine who stays and who goes. In all reorganizations, geography is weighted heavily, along with performance and tenure. Reps that are frequently moving, are not favored in today's environment. Stay with your company, follow the steps in this handbook, make yourself a more valuable employee, and ride out any reorganization.

- **Increase Your Value:** Seek out additional responsibility. Find ways to contribute to the team. Be a volunteer. You might find this excessive, but remember, you do not want to be the average rep. You want to be the best, and one of the best ways to ensure you will not be displaced during reorganization is to increase your value.

- **Be Alert For Opportunity:** You never want to find yourself displaced and without a backup plan. Don't spend worry time wondering the problem excessively, but be prepared for bad corporate news should it come. Stay in touch with the business environment, and keep current on when options within your current company are posted. Many companies have internal websites where positions available within the company are posted. If you feel a need to move into a different field, do not rule out your current organization. If you have been successful in your current position, and have spent the minimum time required in that position, let your DM know your intentions. Most top flight DM's will work hard to help their productive, successful reps move within the company. You might also reach out to recruiters and online associations that provide up to date information on jobs available in the industry. It does not hurt to have your resume on file with these agencies, or pay for an annual subscription to online sites to get the latest information. Table 9 provides an example of some of the recruiters active in this area. This list is not all inclusive.

Table 9: Pharmaceutical Recruiters

Name Of Company	Website
Orion International	www.orioninternational.com
Medical Representatives	www.medreps.com
MBK Worldwide	www.mbkworldwide.com
Dampier Recruiting Association	www.dampierassociates.com
MC Vicker Associates	www.mcvickerassociates.com
PDI Recruiters	www.pdi-inc.com
Healthcare Recruiters	www.hcrnetwork.com
Corbette and Associates	www.corbettandassociates.com
Sales Alliance USA, LLC	www.salesallianceusa.com
The Kenzak Group, Inc.	www.kenzakgroup.com
Carter MacKay	www.cartermackay.com

This table is not all inclusive, there are several recruiters available to help you with your pharmaceutical job search, these are just a few examples of recruiting organizations.

- **Drive Sales:** There is no substitute for throwing big numbers up on the board. This gets positive attention from your DM and above. One of the best ways to secure your future is to be one of the most successful reps in the company. This is no guarantee but, it increases your value and decreases your potential for displacement. Remember, you hold the keys to your future.

☐ **Follow The Industry:** Many companies are shifting their research from the medicines commonly used in family practice and internal medicine to biotechnology, considered by many to be the future for many pharmaceutical companies. Currently, most procedures handled at the family practioner level have several medicines available to deal with a given condition. Most of those medicines have cheaper generic versions. With no new diseases to treat in such an environment, the industry is focusing research on more specialized diseases. Such as, cancers, osteoarthritis, hepatitis C, HIV/Aids. These medicines require a huge amount of research, both laboratory and clinical in the course of developing new products, research that can only be done in the biotechnology environment. Many of these companies will need dedicated, motivated sales representatives with a warrior mentality. Keep yourself up to date on these companies or stay in touch with reps currently working in this area. Stay in touch with recruiters that specialize in placing representatives in these companies.

- **Seek Advice:** The industry is full of great, hard working individuals who have been in sales or management for years. Seek out their advice. When you meet someone who has been with your company for twenty years or more, first congratulate them, and then ask them what they think about the current environment. Ask them what they think about opportunities in other new areas. Striking up a conversation with someone who has been around the industry for years can be an eye opener. Likewise, the current and former District Managers. A person had to do something right to be promoted to DM or higher in this industry. DM's have a track record, and have seen the industry from a variety of vantage points. If you are a successful representative and want to enrich your outlook, ask questions of those who have walked a few miles in a different pair of shoes.

Chapter Wrap: Accepting change, adjusting to it, not panicking at the first sign of trouble, and having a warrior attitude are the tools for survival. This chapter is not designed to strike fear in anyone, only to realistically outline the current landscape and what you can do to stay in touch and survive. Don't ever fool yourself into believing that you are not operating in a high stress environment. You are. That is why you were hired. Just make sure to protect yourself, and make good, sound decisions in the face of change. Follow the points outlined in this chapter and you will better your chances of survival.

Chapter 10

The Future

Many industry observers think that the next few years will bring major, disruptive change to what we call Big Pharma. There are a multitude of classes of medicines available to primary care physicians to treat essentially the same maladies – about two dozen antibiotics alone. Each class of medicine has at least four competitive formulas marketed by separate companies under different trade names. Most of these old reliable medications, including some considered "miracle drugs", are the so called "small molecule" products synthesized from organic chemistry processes. It is these that are at the end of their product life cycle and just a step or two away from going generic, with an accompanying explosive growth in generic manufacturing and sales, and a corresponding decline in the market share of the major pharmaceutical firms in the traditional medicine sectors. That will mean adapting, downsizing, and streamlining for every sector of Big Pharma, even though there are still many small molecule products in their pipelines.

So where does this leave the focus of Research & Development (R&D) in the industry? Currently, according to Intercontinental Marketing Services Health (IMS Health), twenty billion dollars of brand name drugs will face patent expiration in 2008. The industry is pouring more money into R&D than at any other time. 20% of every revenue dollar is funneled back to research. This is a laborious, time consuming, expensive and risky process, yet the industry is willing to accept that expense and risk because of the benefit to people that need these medicines and cures. According to the Pharmaceutical Research and Manufacturers of America (PhRMA), for every ten thousand compounds investigated, perhaps one new drug will make it through the FDA approval process. Gaining approval takes on average, fifteen years of R&D at a cost of eight hundred million dollars. Yet, this does not slow down this amazing industry from pursuing new drugs that will help people and change lives. For example, according to the PhRMA, there are currently two thousand new medicines in the late stages of development. Unfortunately, most Americans believe pharmaceutical drugs comprise a high percentage of the health care dollar. Let's look at the facts. In 2005, the total expenditure on healthcare in the US was two trillion dollars. Of that, 10% or two hundred billion dollars were spent on drugs.

Americans spending two hundred billion dollars on drugs in 2005 sounds expensive. But, can drugs actually save healthcare dollars? You bet! In a study sponsored by the Agency for Health Policy and Research found that increased use of a blood-thinning drug would prevent forty thousand strokes a year at an annual cost savings of six hundred million dollars. Research over the past ten years has shown new HIV/AIDS medicines resulted in a 70% decrease in the mortality rate associated with this disease. This industry is truly making a difference in people's lives.

In the therapeutic area of central nervous system, gastrointestinal disorders, depression, anxiety, high blood pressure, hypertension and others in the infectious disease class, small molecules will continue to dominate, but the shift to the next big thing is irreversible. That new thing will be the "large molecule" products synthesized biologically by live organisms themselves. This new area of R&D focusing on the treatment of cancer and the development of inflammation therapies is being carried out by "biotech" companies. Some of the biotechs are divisions of Big Pharma companies; others are brand new startups. According to PhRMA, in 2007 the industry invested $44.5 billion in R&D. Currently there are 2,700 medicines in the U.S. being developed for over 4,600 indications. There are over 750 medicines that are currently being developed to treat cancer and 547 to treat neurological diseases.

Where's the bad news in this? It depends on where you are. For some, it will be cataclysmic; for others, it will mean moving into areas of unparalleled excitement and opportunity. For those of you new to the industry, or considering entering into a rewarding and exciting profession, you must treat the coming change as akin to the transition from sail to steam or vacuum tube to transistor. American firms and their research laboratories lead the industry, and American innovation will be the wave you want to catch. Regardless of the environment, these companies are adapting and will continue to seek out promising new talent to promote their products competitively in the field. If you are doing well now, if you are a solid performer with a proven track record keep your options open. Stay put if you feel comfortable, but if you plan to enter the industry right out of college, or after getting out of the military you might want to sign on with one of the large companies to gain some experience. If you are a "match" with this industry, you will probably think about a transition into the future boom in biotech pharmaceutical sales.

This is an area poised for an explosion of new products to treat diseases thought "untreatable". It will be a California Gold Rush. The biotech companies that have spent the past decade or so on research and development are delivering at the cusp cures for diseases once simply dreaded, but not cured. The best among you will get on board with one of these companies as soon as possible.

Many of the large pharmaceutical companies have their own Biotech divisions; Draw yourself a roadmap to them and do it quickly. If you are seeking a smaller company feel in the Biotech arena, there are plenty of them out there, doing great work and poised to gain approval for new and novel products. Learn all you can about these companies and position yourself with one of them. 2008-2010 are going to be big years for these companies.

Who will benefit from new technology, these new cures, new biologics and cutting edge procedures almost upon us? Everyone, but especially the baby boomer generation. In the next ten years, the largest segment of the US population will be comprised of people over sixty years old. This aging generation will experience all the ailments and diseases the elderly suffered most from in the past; but, the difference will be that there are cures on the horizon, and those cures will be the product of biotech companies.

- ☐ **The Industry Is Here To Stay:** This amazing industry is here to stay. It was here from the earliest medicine shops over 100 years ago and will be here 100 years from today.

- ☐ **The Industry Is Changing And Will Continue To Change:** Remember, change is good. Prepare for it, follow the steps we have outlined and you will do fine. Don't fight change. If you don't like change, this is not the industry for you. Business and selling models shift constantly. You may be selling cardiovascular drugs one year and central nervous system drugs the next. View change as a challenge to grow as a rep.

- **Go Where The Future Is:** The Biotech Companies are the future. Look internally in your company or outside, but get on board with one of these companies once you have some field experience.

- **Big Pharma:** These companies are going through wrenching change. They will survive, but with smaller sales forces and streamlined products. Change is coming, but remember, these are still great companies to work for and you will need to start with one to gain that valuable sales experience for at least two years, before you move with the new wave of change.

Chapter Wrap: The Pharmaceutical Industry is alive and well, and is here to stay. This industry exists to help people. It provides cures to diseases that destroy lives and families. This industry is on the edge of finding cures for diseases that have plagued humanity since the dawn of history. It is an industry that spends billions of dollars on R&D for new products, cures and medicines that will take us into the biological revolution of the century.

With that said, the industry is going through change, change that will better position it for the future in meeting the needs of people in distress. It's where you want to be, if you're one of the best and the brightest our universities and Armed Services have to offer. It's up to you.

Authors: Todd Bearden and Larry Martin

Todd Bearden

I was hired into Pharmaceutical Sales after retiring from a twenty year career with the US Army. As a soldier, I served the majority of my career in Special Operations and Rapid Deployment Force Units such as, the 75th Ranger Regiment and the 82nd Airborne Division. Serving in numerous leadership positions and extensive military schooling provided me a smooth transition from the US Army to Corporate America. I started my career in Pharmaceutical Sales as a field rep with a large pharmaceutical company. During my career I have sold eight different medicines to a variety of therapeutic specialties in the industry. Additionally, I have been awarded the Presidents Cup for being the top rated sales representative three times, two of which were back to back awards and have received numerous district and region awards while maintaining my position as a top performer year over year. This is an amazing industry and I feel extremely fortunate to be part of it. We want you to share the same success. We wrote this handbook for you. Use it to learn, grow and challenge yourself to go as far as you can in this incredible industry.

Larry Martin

I have been in the industry for twenty eight years, all with the same company. When I started my career, there were only four hundred reps across the company. I have sold numerous medicines spanning several therapeutic classes across several specialties; Hospital, Oncology and Primary Care. Throughout my career, I have been trained on forty plus different drugs and have won national, regional and local awards. I have had the privilege of assisting in training reps over the course of my career and have been called upon to present information at district and regional meetings, to include a presentation before my state committee on Medicaid. The last twenty eight years have been an adventure! I consider myself very lucky to be a part of this wonderful industry, the industry that YOU are now or will soon be a part of. We put this field manual together for YOU! Use it to help you go as far as you can in this amazing industry.

Acronyms

1. Rep or Sales Rep – Short for Pharmaceutical Sales Representative

2. PhRMA - Pharmaceutical Research and Manufacturers of America

3. HCC – Health Care Compliance: Rules that govern the standards of conduct in the industry

4. Presidents Cup – Annual award given to the Top 5% of Pharmaceutical Sales Representatives in the company

5. POD – Group of two, three or four Pharmaceutical Representatives that work for the same company and work in the same territory together as a group

6. DM – District Manager

7. TOP – Territory Organization Plan

8. VP – Vice President

9. CEO – Chief Executive Officer

10. FDA – Food and Drug Administration

11. IMS Health – Intercontinental Marketing Services Health: Provider of business intelligence and strategic consulting services for the pharmaceutical and healthcare industry

12. R & D – Research and Development

13. CMS – Centers for Medicare and Medicaid Services

CPSIA information can be obtained
at www.ICGtesting.com
Printed in the USA
FSOW04n0915221217
42678FS